The Saltville Massacre

CIVIL WAR CAMPAIGNS AND COMMANDERS SERIES

Under the General Editorship of Grady McWhiney

PUBLISHED

Battle in the Wilderness: Grant Meets Lee by Grady McWhiney
Death in September: The Antietam Campaign
        by Perry D. Jamieson
Texans in the Confederate Cavalry by Anne J. Bailey
Sam Bell Maxey and the Confederate Indians by John C. Waugh
The Saltville Massacre by Thomas D. Mays
General James Longstreet in the West: A Monumental Failure
        by Judith Lee Hallock
The Battle of the Crater by Jeff Kinard

FORTHCOMING

Cottonclads! The Battle of Galveston and the Defense of the
        Texas Coast by Donald S. Frazier
A Deep, Steady Thunder: The Battle of Chickamauga
        by Steven E. Woodworth
The Texas Overland Expedition by Richard Lowe
Raphael Semmes and the Alabama by Spencer C. Tucker

The Saltville Massacre

Thomas D. Mays

Under the General Editorship of Grady McWhiney

RYAN PLACE PUBLISHERS
FORT WORTH

Cataloging-in-Publication Data

Mays, Thomas D. 1960—
The Saltville Massacre / Thomas D. Mays.
     p. cm. — (Civil War campaigns and commanders)
    Includes bibliographical references (p.) and index.
    ISBN 1-886661-05-7 (pbk.)

    1. Saltville (Va.)–History, Military. 2. Massacres–Virginia–
Saltville. 3. Afro-American soldiers–Virginia–Saltville–Death.
I. Title. II. Series.
E476.8.M38 1995
973.7'415—dc20

95–23723
CIP

ISBN 1-886661-05-7
10 9 8 7 6 5 4 3 2 1

Book Designed by Rosenbohm Design Group

All inquiries regarding volume purchases of this book should be
addressed to Ryan Place Publishers, Inc., 2525 Arapahoe Avenue,
Suite E4-231, Boulder, CO 80302-6720.

SAN: 298-6779

A Note on the Series

Few segments of America's past excite more interest than
Civil War battles and leaders. This ongoing series of brief,
lively, and authoritative books–*Civil War Campaigns and
Commanders*–salutes this passion with inexpensive and
accurate accounts that are readable in a sitting. Each volume,
separate and complete in itself, nevertheless conveys the
agony, glory, death, and wreckage that defined America's
greatest tragedy.

In this series, designed for Civil War enthusiasts as well as
the newly recruited, emphasis is on telling good stories.
Photographs and biographical sketches enhance the narrative
of each book, and maps depict events as they happened. Sound
history is meshed with the dramatic in a format that is just
lengthy enough to inform and yet satisfy.

Grady McWhiney
General Editor

CONTENTS

CAMPAIGNS AND COMMANDERS SERIES

Map Key

Geography

	Trees
	Marsh
	Fields
	Strategic Elevations
	Rivers
	Tactical Elevations
)ǁ(	Fords
	Orchards
	Political Boundaries

Human Construction

⧂)(	Bridges
┣┽┽┽┽┽┽┽┥	Railroads
	Tactical Towns
● ○	Strategic Towns
□ ■	Buildings
✝	Church
✕	Roads

Military

▬ ▬	Union Infantry
▭ ▭	Confederate Infantry
▱ ▱	Cavalry
ι|ι	Artillery
⚑	Headquarters
△ △△ △ △△ △ △△	Encampments
▷ ⌐	Fortifications
ᒥᒣᒥᒣ	Permanant Works
	Hasty Works
	Obstructions
☆ ✦ ✦ ⚓	Engagements
▬	Warships
▬	Gunboats
▬	Casemate Ironclad
▬	Monitor
	Tactical Movements
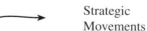	Strategic Movements

**Maps by
Donald S. Frazier, Ph.D.
Abilene, Texas**

MAPS

PHOTOGRAPHS

The brief biographies accompanying the photographs were written by
Grady McWhiney and David Coffey.

The Saltville Massacre

INTRODUCTION

On October 2, 1864, near the southwest Virginia town of Saltville, Confederate forces commanded by General John S. Williams repulsed an invading Union army under General Stephen Gano Burbridge. The battle would have been remembered as a small affair, confined to the footnotes of history books, if it were not for what happened the next morning. What started as a small but intense mountain battle degenerated into a no-quarter racial massacre. Both Union and Confederate eyewitness accounts and regimental records demonstrate that the murders at Saltville were one of the worst atrocities of the Civil War.

Saltville was not the only massacre of black troops in the Civil War. By the end of 1864 battlefield atrocities had become only too common. Confederates were known to have killed Union black prisoners on several occasions, one of the most infamous being at Fort Pillow, Tennessee, on April 12, 1864. But all witnesses agreed that the Federal forces at Fort Pillow had refused to surrender and that Confederates rushing the works granted no quarter to black troops defending the fort.

While Confederate General Nathan Bedford Forrest's actions at Fort Pillow are inexcusable, his men committed the murders during the heat of battle.

The situation at Saltville was quite different. The men killed at Saltville were prisoners, mostly wounded, and were murdered in the days following the fight. Pre-eminent Civil War historian Bell I. Wiley, editor of a Southern account of the executions at Saltville, noted, "It appears that Saltville deserves more than Fort Pillow to be called a massacre."

1
"Captain Fidler's Come to Town"

In the fall of 1864, as General Ulysses S. Grant tightened his noose around the Confederacy, the natural resources of southwest Virginia gained in importance as Southern supplies became scarce. Salt from the area was vital to the Confederates, who depended upon the Virginia and Tennessee Railroad, which ran from Tennessee and points south to Lynchburg and on to Richmond, to distribute it.

Federal General Stephen G. Burbridge pressed for permission to lead an expedition from Kentucky against the saltworks of southwest Virginia. Early in the war Burbridge had done well at the Battle of Shiloh and later was credited with rebuffing John Hunt Morgan's Ohio raid. Yet as commander of the District of Kentucky his inept and tyrannical behavior had alienated most Union supporters. Therefore, the projected expedition was an effort to save his failing reputation.

While General Burbridge planned his invasion the Confederates faced many setbacks. On September 2 General William T. Sherman's forces had captured the vital transportation hub of Atlanta. In Virginia, Confederate General Jubal A. Early's small army operating in the Shenandoah Valley met

View of Saltville, Virginia

stunning defeat at Winchester and Fisher's Hill, thereby opening the way for General Philip H. Sheridan's Union army to
advance up the valley. At Petersburg General Ulysses S. Grant
tightened his headlock on General Robert E. Lee's Army of
Northern Virginia.

In southwest Virginia Confederate General John Echols,

recuperating from wounds, recognized that the fall of Atlanta would free Federal forces for a possible raid on the area. Upon his arrival in the department of southwest Virginia, Echols admitted that he "found everything in the worst possible condition." Many of the troops in the department were unarmed, others were mutinous, and many lacked regimental organization. In addition to the threat of a Federal attack, pro-Union sentiment was strong in both southwest Virginia and in East Tennessee, and the area had become a refuge for hundreds of Confederate deserters. Should the Federals advance, Echols believed he would "have serious fears of the result." Still, during the fall of 1864 Echols did all in his power to organize the defenses in southwest Virginia. He mobilized and reorganized the local reserve forces, noting in the process that they would

Lower salt-works

make good troops "if they had not had the power to select their own officers."

Authorities in Richmond heeded General Echols's warnings. On September 27 Confederate Secretary of War James A. Seddon ordered General John C. Breckinridge to return to southwest Virginia and take personal command. Although a political general, Breckinridge had proven himself a competent

Stephen Gano Burbridge: born Kentucky 1831; attended Georgetown College and the Kentucky Military Institute, becoming a lawyer and plantation owner in Kentucky prior to the Civil War; a staunch Unionist in a state bitterly divided on the secession issue, he accepted a commission as colonel of the 26th Kentucky (US) Infantry; promoted to brigadier general, U.S. Volunteers, in June 1862, he commanded a brigade in the preliminary movements against Vicksburg later that year and was active in the Yazoo expedition, at Chickasaw Bluffs, and in the capture of Arkansas Post; he served credibly throughout the Vicksburg Campaign of 1863, after which he remained on duty in the Department of the Gulf; in April 1864 he assumed direction of the District of Kentucky, Department of the Ohio; brevetted major general of volunteers for his role in repulsing Confederate General John Hunt Morgan's celebrated raid in July 1864; despite this success, Burbridge quickly earned the hatred of most Kentuckians; an administrative demagogue, he routinely penalized citizens for the actions of Rebel guerrillas, compelled farmers and merchants to sell their produce and goods to the Federal government at below market value, and threatened to arrest anyone believed to oppose President Abraham Lincoln's re-election; to help

cover these excesses and to bolster a sinking reputation, Burbridge launched an expedition against the vital Confederate salt mines in southwestern Virginia; in October 1864, after an order from General W.T. Sherman canceling the operation failed to reach him, Burbridge attacked a numerically inferior Confederate force at Saltville, Virginia, and was repulsed; this failure, coupled with his administrative abuses, prompted the general's removal in February 1865; his harsh wartime measures and the lingering animosity of Kentuckians prevented Burbridge from remaining in his native state following the war and forced the relocation of his family to New York. General Burbridge died at Brooklyn in 1894.

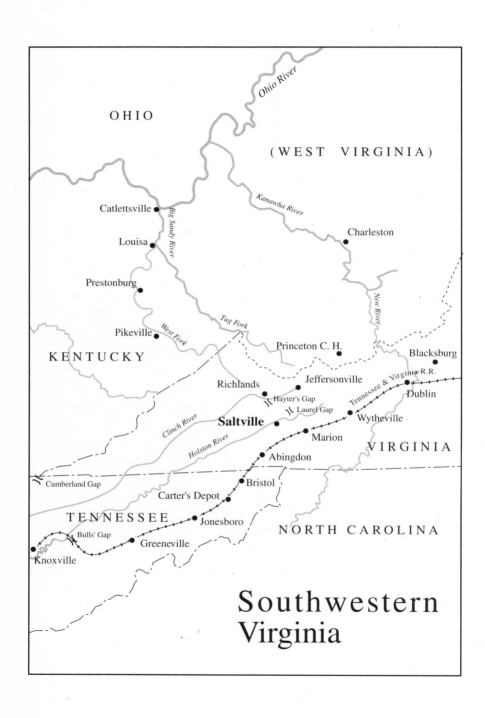

OHIO

Ohio River

(WEST VIRGINIA)

Kanawha River

Catlettsville •

Big Sandy River

Louisa •

Charleston •

Prestonburg •

New River

Tug Fork

Pikeville •

West Fork

KENTUCKY

Princeton C. H. •

Blacksburg •

Richlands •

Jeffersonville •

Tennessee & Virginia R.R.

Dublin •

• Hayter's Gap

• Laurel Gap

Saltville •

Wytheville •

Clinch River

Holston River

Marion •

VIRGINIA

Abingdon •

Cumberland Gap

Bristol •

Carter's Depot •

NORTH CAROLINA

Jonesboro •

TENNESSEE

• Bulls' Gap

Greeneville •

Knoxville •

Southwestern Virginia

military commander. In May 1864 he had saved the Shenandoah Valley from destruction at the Battle of New Market. There his ragtag army, including the cadets of the Virginia Military Institute, had defeated a numerically superior Federal invading army. But by the time Breckinridge was ordered back to the department, the Union Army was already on the move.

On September 20, 1864, the Federal campaign began as the main force of three brigades of Kentucky cavalry and

John Echols: born Virignia 1823; graduated from Washington College (now Washington and Lee); studied law at Harvard, he was admitted to the bar in 1843; before the Civil War he served as the commonwealth's attorney, a member of the general assembly, and a delegate to the secession convention; after recruiting in the western counties, he commanded the 27th Virginia Infantry at First Manassas as a lieutenant colonel, and soon thereafter received promotion to colonel; severely wounded at Kernstown during the Valley Campaign of 1862; Stonewall Jackson described Echols as a "noble leader"; commissioned brigadier general in 1862, poor health plagued him throughout the war; he later serviced almost entirely in western Virginia, except for a brief time at Cold Harbor; participated in numerous actions, including the Battle of New Market; learning that Lee had abandoned Petersburg, Echols collected a force of 7,000 men and marched east to reinforce Lee, who surrendered before Echols arrived; he joined Joseph E. Johnston's army in North Carolina, and fled into Georgia when Johnston surrendered; after the war, General Echols became a prominent businessman in Staunton, Virginia, and Louisville, Kentucky; he helped organize the Chesapeake & Ohio Railway, and served on the board of visitors of the Virginia Military Institute and Washington and Lee University; large in stature, six feet four inches tall and weighing two hundred and sixty pounds, he was said "to have rarely made an enemy and never lost a friend." He died in Staunton in 1896.

mounted infantry headed east from Mount Sterling, Kentucky. Four days later, six hundred men of the new 5th United States Colored Cavalry (USCC) joined Burbridge's army at Prestonburg, Kentucky.

The blacks Burbridge planned to use in the raid would pose a special problem. Even though President Abraham Lincoln's plan for arming ex-slaves to fight their former masters had

Salt Valley

matured by 1864, Kentucky presented a dilemma to the Lincoln administration. It was a "loyal" slave state. The Emancipation Proclamation failed to free any Kentucky slaves; even so many abolitionists pressed for the arming of blacks in the state. Given the difficult task of raising black units for the U.S. government, Adjutant General Lorenzo Thomas took a personal hand in recruiting and was responsible for almost

John C. Breckinridge: born Kentucky 1821; member of an old and honored Bluegrass family; attended Centre College, the College of New Jersey (now Princeton), and studied law at Transylvania University; practiced law briefly in Lexington in 1845; after a short residence in Iowa, he returned to Kentucky and married Mary Cyrene Birch; despite his family's Whig background, he took an interest in Democratic politics; saw no action during the War with Mexico, but vis-

ited Mexico City as major in the 3d Kentucky Volunteers; served in the Kentucky legislature from 1849 to 1851, and in the U.S. House of Representatives from 1851 to 1855; nominated and elected Vice President of the United States on the James Buchanan ticket in 1856, the youngest in American history; in 1859, a year and a half before his term was to expire, he was elected to the U.S. Senate by the Kentucky legislature; in 1860 accepted presidential nomination of the Southern Rights wing of the split Democratic Party; favored southern rights, and when Kentucky declared for the Union in September 1861, he accepted a commission as Confederate brigadier general; in 1862 promoted to major general, commanded the reserve corps at Shiloh, defended Vicksburg, and failed in an attack on Baton Rouge, but fought desperately at Murfreesboro; in 1863 participated in General Joseph Johnston's Campaign to relieve Vicksburg; in 1864 commanded the Department of Southwest Virginia, and accompanied General Jubal Early in the raid on Washington; on February 4, 1865, President Davis appointed him secretary of war; following Confederate surrender, he escaped to Cuba, then to England, and finally to Canada; disclaimed all political ambitions, returned to Kentucky, and resumed his law practice. He died in Lexington, Kentucky, in 1875. "What a handsome and imposing appearance he made! Tall, straight, dignified, he was the ideal Kentuckian among Kentuckians," exclaimed a soldier. "Elegantly appareled, wearing the full dress uniform of a Confederate major-general, his bearing was indeed knightly. Boys, he'll do…, ain't he grand?" General Robert E. Lee considered Breckinridge a "lofty, pure, strong man…a great man."

half of the black regiments raised.

In early 1864 General Burbridge issued General Order No. 24, which authorized the raising of black units composed of freedmen and exslaves. The order admitted slaves at the "request" of their owners. Whites in the state reacted violently to the arming of their former slaves. Captain James Fidler, an enlisting officer in Lebanon, Kentucky, witnessed his black recruits mobbed and beaten in the streets. When the white 13th Kentucky Cavalry arrived in Lebanon early in June, Fidler found that he, too, was a target for violence; on June 10 he narrowly missed being killed by a shot fired at him by a sniper in the town. Later one of Fidler's black recruits recorded his experience in verse:

Captain Fidler's come to town,
    With his abolition papers;
He swears he is one of Lincoln's men,
    He's cutting almighty capers.

Captain Fidler's come to town,
    With his abolition triggers,
He swears he's one of Lincoln's men,
    "Enlisting all the niggers."...

You'll see the rebels on the street,
    Their noses like a bee gum;
I Don't care what in thunder they say,
    I'm fighting for my freedom!...

My old massa's come to town,
    Cutting a Southern figure;
What's the matter with the man?
    Lincoln's got his niggers?

Some folks say this "almighty fuss
    Is getting worse and bigger";
Some folks say "its worse and worse,"
    Because I am a "nigger."

We'll get our colored regiments strung
    Out in a line of battle;
I'll bet my money agin the South
    The rebels will skedaddle.

Pressure on recruiting officers began to ease in the state when the white population realized that black units would help offset Kentucky's draft quota. The Federals took advantage of the opportunity by ordering slaves in the state to be enrolled without regard to the wishes of their owners. On June 30 Adjutant General Thomas gave permission for the officers of the 5th USCC to start selecting recruits for the regiment.

Colonel James Brisbin, a well-known abolitionist, eventually became commander of the 5th USCC. His first duty with the unit was as head of Camp Nelson, a camp of instruction south of Louisville, where he trained the new volunteers for the regiment. The work proceeded slowly in the summer and fall of 1864. Many of the companies of the regiment were recruited at Camp Nelson, while others were enlisted in nearby towns including Lebanon and Louisville.

With only a handful of free skilled workers, the regiment consisted almost entirely of ex-slaves. The majority were volunteers who had enlisted for three years, but one company became a dumping ground for draftees and conscripts. Of eighty-three men in Company L, fifty-three were substitutes and ten were draftees.

Under Thomas's organizational plans the officers of the 5th USCC were to be whites selected by a board; the noncommissioned officers were to be chosen from black men in the ranks. Yet with an entire regiment consisting mainly of ex-slaves, the officers found it difficult to find men literate enough to handle the tasks assigned to sergeants. Lieutenant Colonel L. Henry Carpenter asked for permission to appoint experienced white soldiers as noncommissioned officers. "Scarcely any of the Coloredmen [sic] enlisted into this regiment can read or write," he stated. It would be months before the regiment would be able to train the men it needed for efficient operation.

While many Kentuckians continued to harass Federal authorities in their efforts to recruit black troops, some white officers made matters worse. Captain Thomas Bunch of the 5th USCC contributed to the problem by confiscating slaves for the regiment and then accepting bribes from their owners for their return; the usual "tariff" was one hundred dollars, and Bunch threatened many slave owners with violence if they failed to accept his terms. He then gave the slaves' enlistment papers to the owners and kept the slaves for the regiment. Bunch was eventually punished, but not before he had alienated many "loyal" Kentuckians.

When word reached them of the impending expedition, the men of the 5th USCC still had not been organized into a regiment. Some had not even enlisted; only a few of their officers had been appointed, and even fewer noncommissioned officers were at their posts. Command of the group went to Colonel James F. Wade, who would eventually command the 6th USCC. With the assistance of Colonel James Brisbin, the officers hastily attempted to organize an untrained mob of recruits into some semblance of order. The men of the 5th were issued Enfield infantry rifles (weapons useless to mounted men as they could not be loaded from horseback), and untrained horses.

Upon joining Burbridge's force at Prestonburg, Kentucky, Brisbin observed that his men "were made the subject of much ridicule and many insulting remarks by the white troops, and in some instances petty outrages, such as pulling off the caps of the colored soldiers, stealing their horses etc." While it was common for veteran regiments to tease green troops, the harassment of the 5th USCC had ugly racial overtones. Brisbin concluded that "these insults, as well as the jeers and taunts that they would not fight, were borne by the colored soldiers patiently. . . . In no instance did I hear colored soldiers make any reply to insulting language used toward [them] by white troops."

2
"GRAVE YARD WHISTLING"

Burbridge's plan called for three separate columns. He would march directly on the saltworks with General Nathaniel C. McLean's Kentucky Division while the other two columns created a diversion. Burbridge personally took command of McLean's Division of mounted infantry, cavalry, and mountain howitzers–in all over 4,000 men. General Jacob Ammen with 800 troops was to hold Bull's Gap, Tennessee, blocking the Virginia and Tennessee Railroad, while General Alvan C. Gillem advanced on Jonesboro, Tennessee, with 1,650 men. Ammen and Gillem would then link up and join Burbridge for the raid on Saltville.

On September 27 Burbridge's army left Prestonburg, advanced through Pikeville, pushed a small party of Confederate pickets from its path, and camped for the night. Here Burbridge prepared his men for the rough passage through the mountains of southwest Virginia. He ordered the

Alvan C. Gillem: born Tennessee 1830; graduated from the U.S. Military Academy in 1851, eleventh in his class of forty-two; posted to artillery and commissioned 2d lieutenant, he saw service in Florida and on the Texas frontier; promoted to 1st lieutenant in March 1855 and captain in May 1861; following the outbreak of the Civil War he remained in the regular army, becoming assistant quartermaster in July 1861; as chief quartermaster to Generals George Thomas and Don Carlos Buell he was present at Mill Springs, Shiloh, and Corinth; transferring to the volunteer organization, he was commissioned colonel of the 10th Tennessee (US) Infantry in May 1862; Gillem served as provost marshal at Nashville from August to December 1862; in June 1863 he was appointed adjutant general of Tennessee by Military Governor Andrew Johnson; promoted to brigadier general of volunteers in August 1863; given command of a cavalry division in the Army of the Cumberland, he divided his time between field service and the reorganization of Tennessee's state government; in July 1864 Gillem's troopers killed celebrated Confederate raider John Hunt Morgan in eastern Tennessee; he participated in numerous raids in Tennessee, North Carolina, and southwestern Virginia, being conspicuously engaged while commanding a division in General George Stoneman's raid in the winter of 1864–65; brevetted through major general in the regular army, Gillem was promoted to full major general of vol-

unteers at the close of hostilities; he was mustered out of the volunteer organization in September 1866; he continued in the regular army first as colonel of the 28th Infantry and then as colonel of the 1st Cavalry; he earned criticism for his lenient application of reconstruction policy while heading the Fourth Military District (Arkansas and Mississippi); returning to the frontier, he saw his final action in northern California; in 1873, although desperately ill, he helped direct the suppression of Captain Jack's Modoc Indians after the slaying of General E.R.S. Canby; shortly thereafter, his health deteriorating, General Gillem went on sick leave never to return to active duty. He died at Nashville in 1875.

baggage train to the rear; each horse was then loaded with two bushels of corn to be carried behind the saddle. Burbridge's mounted force traveled without wagons or ambulances; mules carried the six small mountain howitzers that served as artillery.

During the next four days Confederates in Colonel Henry L. Giltner's small Kentucky Cavalry Brigade did all in its power to slow the Federal advance. Giltner's command consisted of the 4th Kentucky Cavalry, 10th Kentucky Cavalry, 10th Kentucky Mounted Rifles, 64th Virginia Mounted Infantry, and two unattached companies. In all, Giltner had about three hundred men available to slow Burbridge's four thousand man division. While most of the soldiers were veterans of Morgan's famous

Henry L. Giltner: born Kentucky 1829?; entered the Confederate army at Munfordville, Kentucky, in September 1861, joining the Buckner Guards as a private;

soon General Humphrey Marshall assigned him to duty as aide-de-camp on his staff, and in July 1862 sent him together with several others "upon the hazardous service of recruiting"; because the state was full of Federal troops, "before the party reached the bluegrass region, all except Giltner [and three others]…concluded that the enterprise was fraught with too many dangers, and declined to go any further"; promoted to colonel and given command of the 4th Kentucky Cavalry in October 1862, he "was a lithe, graceful man, of dignified mien, slightly above medium height, symmetrically proportioned, dark complexion, hair and beard black as the raven's wing, gray eyes, and about thirty-three years old"; always "neatly attired, and when he became colonel of the Fourth Kentucky always wore the full and handsome uniform of his rank, and rode a magnificent dapple-gray charger—his old war horse 'Billy'"; "cool, collected, absolutely impervious to excitement, he was a man of dauntless bravery and wonderful fortitude; a strict disciplinarian, yet kind of heart; never effusive nor demonstrative in affection, cavalry, some were less than dependable. Only a month before, Giltner had complained that the 64th Virginia had a desertion rate of over 50 percent and had become completely insubordinate.

The command marched from Abingdon, Virginia, to Clinch Mountain in order to block the Union advance. On September 26, Colonel Giltner received word from General Echols on the Federal movement. Echols also informed Giltner that the Union force included "600 Yankee Negroes [sic]." Confederate Captain Edward O. Guerrant of the 4th Kentucky Cavalry noted in his diary that "these great preparations indicate an invasion on a scale surpassing anything yet undertaken [by the Federals into southwest Virginia]." Giltner then sent the 10th

he nevertheless concerned himself more for the comfort of his troops than any other commander I ever knew," wrote George Dallas Mosgrove. "Belonging to his military family, I understood him thoroughly and know whereof I write. A soft voice and an easy flow of language made him an entertaining companion, and yet, his dignified bearing and a peculiarity, natural to him, of 'carrying his head high,' impressed not a few with the mistaken idea that he was cold and exclusive. Under his quiet exterior was a vein of humor, and no man had a higher appreciation of the humorous and ludicrous than he." General John Echols, in recommending him for promotion to brigadier general, wrote: "Colonel Giltner...has always discharged his duty most faithfully and efficiently....For nearly two years...he has been in command of a brigade, and has shown himself on all occasions fully equal to the position, both in the discipline of his men and in handling them on the field of battle. He is a rigid disciplinarian, always having his command well in hand, looking to their wants and promoting their efficiency." Colonel Giltner died in 1891 at Murfreesboro, Tennessee. A staff officer wrote: "Henry Giltner was a man among men. No man ever commanded truer, braver men than his old regiment. They chose him because of the sterling qualities which he possessed in a rare degree. It was not because he was a great man; he was not; not because he was a learned man; his education was very limited; not because he was a trained soldier; he knew but little of military tactics or the art of war; but he possessed what was better than all these virtues–character. If I were asked why this humble, uneducated countryman rose to eminent distinction among the best and bravest men I ever knew, I would say, *character.*"

Edward O. Guerrant: born Kentucky; son of a physician, he was "a bright, handsome young man, Chesterfieldian in manner, possessing wondrous fluency of speech"; graduated from Centre College; small in stature, but "a conspicuous figure in any assemblage" and as "polite as the politest Frenchman, gentle and refined as any lady," said a friend–"a superb cavalier, intrepid as Henry of Navarre, from whose sunny France he had descended"; he served during the war as adjutant-general on the staff of General John S. Williams and Colonel Henry Giltner

with the rank of captain; "faultlessly...attired" and always "fastidious about the work," he was "a voluminous prose writer, and also wrote and quoted a great deal of poetry; his vocabulary seemed to be co-extensive with an unabridged dictionary, and with ease and facility he constructed sentences containing the purest gold of the English language"; regardless of the weather, recalled a clerk, Captain Guerrant "and his horse invariably appeared as if ready to go on dress parade or to pass inspection"; in a parlor "filled with ladies and gentlemen, the captain was generally the cynosure of attention and the charmingly fascinating monopolizer of the conversation"; the more ladies the better, and if there "was a mirror in the room, he was likely to walk to it, brush his hair and arrange his necktie, talking volubly and entertainingly all the while. Such procedure would have been ludicrously grotesque in any other man, but with the adjutant-general it seemed to be the correct thing to do, and no one thought of criticizing his peculiar movements; his grace, his wit and vivacity charmed his auditors, who, unquestioningly, gave him *carte blanche* to do as he pleased"; his "conversational powers were unrivaled–fluent, didactic, oratorical, and witty"; his friends believed that after the war he would become "a magnificent lawyer," but instead he studied medicine in Philadelphia until he decided "that it was his duty to employ his gifted mind and rare accomplishments in preaching his Master's gospel, which profession he...followed with the same vigor and success that characterized his former undertakings. His eloquent voice has been heard throughout Kentucky and in many of the Southern States."

Kentucky Mounted Rifles to picket the Richlands and Fincastle crossroads and the old courthouse at Russell.

Colonel Giltner remained at his headquarters near Hayter's Gap for the next several days. On September 27, several members of the brigade reached headquarters from Kentucky. They informed the command of the latest atrocities in their home state. Burbridge had "ordered that anyone *Traveling* by *night* should be fired on as a Thief or a robber." The men of Giltner's Kentucky Brigade had many personal scores to settle with Burbridge. What they faced was no unknown army from the North, but Kentucky Union troops. The Yankees were their neighbors, relatives, and ex-slaves; any fight would likely become a personal affair. In any case, Giltner's men remained far from optimistic. They knew that their little three-hundred-man brigade could do little to slow Burbridge's thousands. Giltner also received word that more local militia were being summoned up and that General Williams's cavalry Brigade would soon be in Virginia. One overoptimistic message ended by stating: "everything working well as Great resources in Dept...." After reading the dispatch and receiving more information on the scope of the Federal advance, one young Rebel passed off the optimistic talk as being little more than "Grave Yard Whistling."

On the night of September 29, the Federal force crested Laurel Mountain. A severe storm battered the column. Captain Mason of the 12th Ohio Cavalry reported that "the horrors of that night march eclipsed all previous experiences of the regiment." With treacherous footing and zero visibility, the path across Laurel Mountain became perilous to soldiers and their mounts. Mason added that "from time to time a hapless horse would step beyond the narrow brink, and a cry of despair, followed by a dull crash many feet below would be the only requiem of beast and rider. In this way eight men were lost." Several others were rescued with ropes.

Colonel Giltner did all he could to slow the Federals.

During the night he attempted to reinforce his pickets by sending Colonel Edward Trimble's 10th Kentucky Cavalry with 150 men through the storm to Richlands. On the morning of the thirtieth, the Union army rested until noon before resuming its advance. Giltner used the opportunity to withdraw his command back to Liberty Hill. He also prepared for the worst by sending his extra horses, cattle, and baggage train south of the Virginia and Tennessee Railroad, so as to protect his supplies in case the brigade should be outflanked.

That afternoon Trimble's small command attempted to make a stand and was quickly brushed aside. At the next gap Trimble was again overrun and Giltner then consolidated his entire brigade at the foot of Clinch Mountain near the farm of militia General Reese T. Bowen.

That night Giltner left Guerrant at headquarters near Bowen's farm and departed for Clinch Mountain. Around midnight Guerrant was awakened by the sound of gunfire from the direction of the farm. Knowing that untrained reserves were at Bowen's, Guerrant decided to ignore the firing, chalking it up to nervous and inexperienced militia. Yet the gunfire soon increased, and Guerrant shortly received the order to move out. Federal troops had overrun Giltner's Brigade in the darkness.

The militia managed to kill at least one Federal before falling back. Guerrant then retreated up Clinch Mountain and sent word to Giltner of the attack. He also attempted to recall all the pickets, but Captain Jenkins's Company would remain cut off from the rest of the Confederate forces for the next two days. The Federals halted at Bowen's for the night. Aware that Bowen commanded some of the militia in the area, the Yankees stripped his farm of food and forage.

The next morning, the Southerners awakened in the rain to find Burbridge's army in full view in the valley below them. Guerrant used his telescope to watch the Federals as they continued to loot Bowen's farm and cook their breakfast. He estimated the size of the Union force and noted that it included "400 negro soldiers." Giltner used the early morning hours to deploy his small brigade. The road going up Clinch Mountain takes a cutback course with many zig zags as it travels up the northwestern face of the mountain. Giltner sent the 10th Kentucky Cavalry to the next gap and dismounted the remainder of the brigade along the side of the mountain. The colonel then placed the 64th Virgina on the flank while the 4th and 10th Kentucky Mounted Rifles held the road.

At 9 A.M. Burbridge left camp and advanced toward the foot of Clinch Mountain. One Confederate, George Dallas

George Dallas Mosgrove: born Kentucky 1844; his father, a native of Pennsylvania, was a carpenter, who in 1850 owned real estate valued at $800; as demonstrated by his post-war writings, George Mosgrove received a good education; his penmanship, a widely practiced nineteenth century art, was outstanding; in 1862 he enlisted in the 4th Kentucky Cavalry, and remained a private throughout the war; he might have received a higher rank by transferring to another unit, but he preferred being a private in what he considered an elite organization to being an officer in a more "ordinary" outfit; early in his service, he served as clerk and orderly at regimental headquarters; later he moved up to brigade headquarters and assisted the adjutant as copyist and messenger, which gave him considerable freedom of movement and enabled him to meet persons of high rank; after the war, Mosgrove settled near Carrollton, Kentucky, but information about him is scant; he became a teacher in a one-room public school and wrote a number of articles about the 4th Kentucky; he married twice, and died in 1907 near Carrollton. A contemporary described him as a truthful, gentle, "honorable man, of medium height, rather nice-looking, not much of a joker, but a good talker, with an almost perfect command of the English language." His reminiscences of *Kentucky Cavaliers in Dixie*, edited by Bell I. Wiley in 1957 and reprinted in 1991, first appeared in 1895.

Mosgrove of the 4th Kentucky Cavalry, was impressed at the Union approach. "The long, blue columns as they debouched from their camps made a magnificent panoramic display. On they came on a serpentine course, bugles sounding and panoplied in all the pomp and circumstance of war." Knowing that they comprised the only force between Burbridge and Saltville, the three-hundred-man force of Giltner's command realized that they had to slow the Federal advance until more support could arrive.

At 10 A.M. the head of the Federal column came within range of the Confederate line. A quick volley emptied several saddles and sent the head of the column scurrying off to dismount and prepare to fight on foot. The Federals reorganized, advanced, and opened fire on the Confederates in the cut-back road above them. The skirmish continued at a distance of three hundred yards with little progress made by either side. After half an hour, Giltner ordered his Confederate Brigade to fall back.

The Confederates retreated to the crest of Flat Top Mountain and dismounted again astride the road. Giltner placed the 64th Virginia and 10th Kentucky Cavalry across the main road and sent the 4th Kentucky Cavalry and 10th Kentucky Mounted Rifles along a second approach. At 2 P.M. the Federals attacked again. Giltner's Brigade held its position until the dismounted Federals overran the Confederate left flank. This time the Confederates retreated to Laurel Gap (known today as Low Gap). This was their final position of the day.

At Laurel Gap, Giltner found Colonel Robert H. Smith's militia Battalion from Tazewell guarding the position. Giltner ordered Smith and his 250 "old men & boys" to guard the smaller gaps toward the saltworks while he organized his command for a third stand. Guerrant described the gap as "the strongest natural position in this country; but like all others liable to be flanked."

The gap is a narrow gorge surrounded on each side by high cliffs. On the left side of the gap, Giltner stationed the 4th Kentucky Cavalry and 10th Kentucky Mounted Rifles; on the right he posted the 64th Virginia. Finally, Giltner sent Trimble's 10th Kentucky Cavalry down the valley behind the mountains to prevent the brigade from being cut off from the saltworks in case they were flanked.

Around 5 P.M. the Federals arrived at the gap. This time they lost no time in dismounting and assaulting the position. Once again the Northerners had no intention of scaling the cliffs directly in front. They held their position and sent a flanking force around the Confederate right. The 37th Kentucky (Federal) Mounted Infantry took the lead in a flank attack on the 64th Virginia Mounted Infantry. The Virginia unit lived up to its poor reputation and ran from the field. In the attack the 37th lost one man killed and several wounded as Giltner's entire Brigade then fell back in the direction of Saltville.

By the night of October 1, the Federals had pushed Giltner's men within two miles of Saltville. The town had only Giltner's Brigade and the local milita to protect it. Yet instead of immediately attacking and capturing the saltworks before reinforcements arrived, Burbridge ordered his men to camp for the night.

During the day in Saltville, the Virginia militia attempted to organize. Upon arriving in town, seventeen-year-old Second Lieutenant John H. Wise joined Colonel Robert T. Preston's militia Battalion. Wise had attended Virginia Military Institute and had seen combat with the cadets at the Battle of New Market. Later, using his father's political connections as ex-governor and general, Wise secured a commission in the Virginia militia. When Wise reported to Colonel Preston, he found that "Colonel Bob" was "short, thick-set, and had an immense snow-white beard, extending nearly to his sword-belt." Wise concluded that Preston's "appearance, figure

Alfred E. "Mudwall" Jackson: born Tennessee 1807; attended Washington and Greenville colleges; farmed the Nolichucky River area of East Tennessee; afterwards became a wholesaler and merchant; energetic and ambitious, he traded all over the South, using wagons and boats to transport his merchandise; by the 1850s his enterprises—stores, farms, sawmills, and gristmills—crossed Tennessee from the Smoky Mountains to the Mississippi River; in 1861 Jackson entered Confederate service as a quartermaster with the rank of major, serving on the staff of General Felix K. Zollicoffer until that officer's death; subsequently Jackson served as paymaster in Knoxville; in response to petitions from hundreds of citizens and pressure from congressmen, he was called to Richmond in 1863, appointed brigadier general, and assigned to the command of an infantry brigade in the Department of East Tennessee; his job was guarding the strategic East

Tennessee and Virginia Railroad linking Chattanooga with Richmond and controlling local Unionists; the new commander of the department, General Simon B. Buckner, redefined Jackson's mission: his troops were to be distributed at the various defenses of the bridges, in minimum garrisons, with the cavalry of the brigade used for scouting and policing roads; with his command General Jackson participated in a number of minor engagements, including the capture of the 100th Ohio Infantry at Telford's Depot in September 1863, an exploit that won him the sobriquet of "Mudwall"; an enlisted man reported, "the boys facetiously called [their commander] 'Mudwall' Jackson in contradistinction to the immortal 'Stonewall'.... General 'Mudwall' being rather slow and wavering"; in the winter of 1863-64, he employed his under-strength command pursuing bushwhackers in the area south of the French Broad River; in September 1864 Jackson rushed to Saltville, Virginia, and took initial command of the defense that repulsed the Yankee attack; Jackson's health failed; he was declared unfit for field duty; never paroled, he probably just went home; ruined economically by the war, General Jackson rented land in Washington County, Virginia, in 1866 and undertook its cultivation with his own hands; subsequently issued a special pardon by President Andrew Johnson for kindness shown his family during the war; Jackson's estates were gradually restored to him, and he was able to take up residence at Jonesboro, Tennessee, where he died in 1889.

beard, merry twinkling eye, and ruddy face instantly suggested Santa Claus." As for Preston's troops, they were in "every stage of manhood, from immature boyhood to decrepit old age. One of his companies drawn up in line looked as irregular as a pile of barrel-hoops. There was no pretense of uniform; they wore everything, from straw hats to coon-skin caps." Their Belgian rifles and cartridge boxes provided the units' only vestige of military appearance.

General William T. Sherman: born Ohio 1820; graduated from U.S. Military Academy 1840, sixth in his class; 2d lieutenant 3rd Artillery 1840; 1st lieutenant 1841; stationed in California during Mexican War; captain 1850. Resigned from army 1853 to become banker; after business failed, Sherman voluntarily assumed personal financial responsibility for money lost by his friends; practiced law for a short time in Kansas, losing only case he tried; from 1859 to 1861 superintendent of military college that later became Louisiana State University. Colonel 13th Infantry and then brigadier general volunteers 1861; commanded brigade at First Bull Run; commanded division at Shiloh; major general volunteers 1862 to 1864, serving under Grant in the Vicksburg and Chattanooga campaigns; brigadier general U.S. Army 1863; major general 1864; assumed direction of principal military operations in the West. Directed Meridian and Atlanta campaigns, March to the Sea, and Carolina campaign that ended in surrender of Joseph E. Johnston's army in 1865; received thanks of Congress "for gallant and arduous services" during the Civil War; lieutenant general 1866; general 1869; commander of the army 1869 to 1883; retired 1883; published memoirs 1875; died 1891. Made his famous statement, "war is all hell," in a  speech at Columbus, Ohio, in 1880. An officer noted that Sherman's "features express determination, particularly the mouth. He is a very homely man, with a regular nest of wrinkles in his face, which play and twist as he eagerly talks on each subject; but his expression is pleasant and kindly." Some authorities rate him an even better general than Grant.

That evening Colonel Preston reported to General Alfred E. "Mudwall" Jackson in Saltville. When Preston arrived, the general said: "Kernel, …my men tell me the Yanks have a lot of nigger soldiers along. Do you think your reserves will fight niggers?"

"Fight'em?" replied Preston, "by ____, Sir, they'll eat'em up! No! Not eat'em up! That's too much! By ____, Sir, we'll cut'em up!"

Like Burbridge, Federal General Gillem's force enjoyed success on October 1. Gillem had united with Ammen's command in order to push the Confederates from Jonesboro, Tennessee. After a brief skirmish at Jonesboro on September 29, the Federals pushed John Vaughn's Confederate command back to Carter's Station on the Watauga River. On October 1 Gillem forced the Confederates from their works along the river. He was preparing to join Burbridge's main force at Saltville when a courier arrived with word that Confederate General Nathan

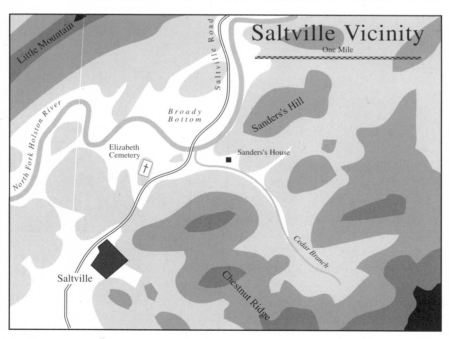

Bedford Forrest was threatening Sherman's supply line to Atlanta. Sherman canceled Burbridge's entire operation and ordered him into Tennessee to block Forrest. Gillem immediately started for Tennessee, but Burbridge would not receive the order for another two days.

Perhaps Burbridge was content that night to rest upon his laurels. He had just crossed some of the most rugged terrain in the East, and had gotten closer to the saltworks than any previous Union commander. Although opposed by Colonel Giltner's veterans, Burbridge had easily brushed all resistance aside. The next morning, Burbridge expected to find only the remnants of Giltner's beaten Brigade along with the local militia. He had no reason to anticipate much resistance from the "old men and boys" of southwest Virginia.

3

"WE SURELY SLEW NEGROES THAT DAY."

A cold and foggy morning greeted both sides as they prepared for the impending struggle. General Burbridge's hopes were high. As far as he knew, the only Confederate troops between his army and the saltworks were Giltner's weary command and the local militia. Yet even as his Federals were cooking their breakfast, the Confederates were reinforcing Saltville.

In all, the Rebels assembled about 2,800 troops to face 4,500 Federals. The Southerners had been reinforced by General John S. Williams, who took personal command of the defense of Saltville and placed his cavalry Division with the other troops defending the hills surrounding town. Yet Burbridge never deployed his full force; instead he made several piecemeal attacks on the Confederate works without ever bringing into battle more than 2,500 men at one time.

John S. Williams: born Kentucky 1818; graduated from Miami University 1839; admitted to the bar the following year; commenced practicing law in Paris, Kentucky, in 1840; during the Mexican War he served first as captain of an independent company attached to the 6th U.S. Infantry, and later as colonel of the 4th Kentucky Volunteers; led his regiment in the assault on the heights at Cerro Gordo, which won him the nickname by which he was afterwards known—"Cerro Gordo"; resumed his law practice and raised cattle after the war; a Whig member of the Kentucky legislature in 1851 and 1853, he had been anti-secessionist until coercion by the Federal government changed his mind; ultimately he entered the Confederate Army in 1861 as colonel of the 5th Kentucky Infantry; in 1862 promoted to brigadier general, he skirmished with the enemy in the Cumberland Gap region; during that time Major General W.W. Loring described Williams as "energetic and valuable"; after participating in the Kentucky Campaign of 1862, he commanded a brigade in southwest Virginia until September 1863, when he opposed General Ambrose Burnside's advance toward Knoxville; badly outnumbered, Williams nevertheless fought fiercely at Blue Springs, beating off several attacks and bluffing the enemy by using three locomotives to simulate the arrival of reinforcements; Williams displayed courage and energy during his retreat to Virginia; disgusted that his superiors saw his actions only as a defeat, he gave up command in East Tennessee at his own request and was stationed in southwest Virginia until attached in 1864 to General Joseph Wheeler's Cavalry Corps in the Army of Tennessee; while raiding in Tennessee in August, Williams persuaded Wheeler to let him take two brigades and some artillery to attack a Federal post at Strawberry Plains, but when Williams failed to reach his objective, Wheeler censured him in his report; Williams tranferred to southwestern Virginia for the remainder of the war; returning to farming at Winchester, Kentucky, he served in the state legislature in 1873 and 1875, and was an unsuccessful candidate for governor; elected to the United States Senate, in 1878, but failed to be re-elected. He died at Mount Sterling, Kentucky, in 1898.

The Federals began the battle by pushing Giltner's Brigade back to the main Confederate line, which followed the rough terrain surrounding Saltville. Northeast of town, Sanders's Hill and Chestnut Ridge dominate the area. Between the two hills runs Cedar Branch, a small stream in a deep ravine that passes close to "Governor" James Sanders's house and empties into the North Fork of the Holston River near the river road ford. The Southerners occupied postitions on Chestnut Ridge behind Sanders's house, and they had fortified the yard of a small log church to the left of the ford near Elizabeth Cemetery.

As Giltner's men passed through the Southern line they found four hundred old men and boys of Colonel Robert H. Smith's 13th Battalion of Virginia Reserves from Smyth, Washington, Tazewell, and Russell counties. The reserves were barricading themselves in Sanders's house, located halfway

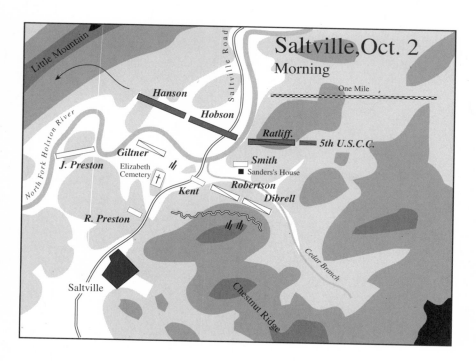

down a steep ravine leading to Cedar Branch. Giltner attempted to entice Smith's men to join him but the reserves refused
and resolved to stand their ground.

After pushing in Giltner's Brigade, Federals concentrated
their efforts on Smith's exposed position at Sanders's house.
The sixty-year-old Sanders, known locally as "Governor"
because of his position in the community, joined the reserves
outside his house. His wife and children barricaded themselves inside in a large fireplace, using feather mattresses and
pillows to cover the opening.

Soon, over two thousand Federals charged and over-
whelmed Smith's exposed command. Attacking in three
columns, with both mounted and dismounted troops, the
Federals overran the reserves at the house. The scene amazed
all who witnessed it. The motley colletion of militia, who were
hardly expected to fight, attempted to hold their ground and
even engaged in hand-to-hand fighting with the Federals. One
witness noted that the reserves fought with "more courage
than prudence" before they fell back to the main Confederate
line. Another Southern veteran remembered that it was one of
the most stubborn conflicts he had ever witnessed. He "beheld
gray-haired men and fair-haired boys lying side by side pale in
death, slain at the threshold of their homes, on their native
Virginia soil."

Although the fighting riddled the Sanders's home, the family remained unharmed in its fortified fireplace. The Governor
became a prisoner and his captors brought him before
General Burbridge. When the General asked Sanders what
unit had occupied his property, the answer amazed him.
Burbridge refused to believe that it was only the local men of
Smith's reserves. The four hundred reserves in the 13th
Battalion lost eighty-five men killed, wounded, and missing in
the action.

The next attack came on the Confederate right along
Chestnut Ridge. About halfway up, the Confederates had dug a

series of rifle pits, their main works being along the crest of the ridge. The attack on the forward line came as the Federals continued their advance down Sanders's Hill and up Chestnut Ridge in front of Felix H. Robertson's and George D. Dibrell's small brigades. The battle began in earnest at around 10 A.M. as the Federals made a series of dismounted charges upon Chestnut Ridge. After seeing the strength of the Confederate position, the Yankees decided to attack on foot. After two unsuccessful attempts to take the works, Robert Ratliff's Brigade prepared to make a final charge. This time the 5th USCC, 12th Ohio Cavalry, and 11th Michigan Cavalry would make a dismounted assault up the hill.

Accounting for horse holders and stragglers, around four hundred men of the 5th USCC fell in line with the rest of the brigade. The 5th assembled on the Federal left. As the Federal battle line formed, Dibrell's Confederate scouts could hear a speech given to Ratliff's Brigade by an officer whom they

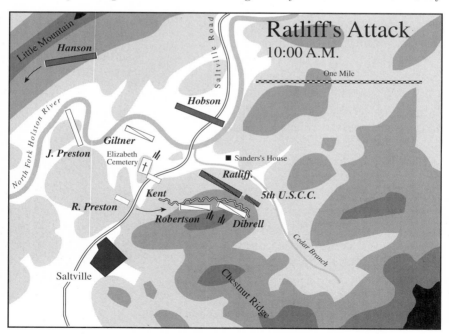

assumed to be Burbridge. The officer encouraged the men in their efforts and stated that depriving the Confederates of the saltworks would do more to bring down the Confederacy than the capture of Richmond.

Ratliff's Brigade advanced down an overgrown ravine behind Sanders's farm, crossed Cedar Branch, and then moved up Chestnut Ridge. Confederate and Federal skirmishers met in the dense undergrowth in the ravine. One Federal observed: "More than once duels took place between individuals at a distance of not more than half-a-dozen paces—each firing at a noise heard beyond until a groan or a cessation of the firing announced that the heard but unseen enemy was dead. At other times a Rebel would pop out from behind a tree or rock only a few feet from an advancing Yankee, and then it was the quickest and surest shot of the two who lived to tell the story."

Sergeant Jeremiah Davis, the guidon bearer for Company

Robert Wilson Ratliff: an Ohio native, Ratliff began his Civil War service as lieutenant colonel of the 2d Ohio Cavalry; after seeing limited action in the Trans-Mississippi, he resigned in June 1863; returning to duty in October, he joined the 12th Ohio Cavalry as lieutenant colonel and was elevated to colonel the following month; in August 1864 he was given command of the Fourth Brigade, District of Kentucky; in General Stephen Burbridge's October 1864 raid on Saltville, Virginia, Ratliff's mounted brigade included black troopers from the partially formed 5th and 6th United States Colored Cavalry; despite initial success, Ratliff's advance at Saltville was halted by stiff Confederate resistance and a shortage of ammunition; dozens of wounded black soldiers that were captured or left on the field perished in the massacre that followed the battle; Ratliff was brevetted brigadier general of volunteers for his actions at Saltville and subsequent operations in southwestern Virginia and North Carolina under General George Stoneman; he died in 1887.

H, 12th Ohio Cavalry, found himself in a hand-to-hand fight for his colors with a Confederate. With no help in sight, and only the flag for a weapon, Davis "harpooned his enemy with the sharp spear head of the flagstaff–the brazen point passing through the rebel and appearing between his lower ribs on the opposite side." After much close-in fighting, the Federals emerged from the undergrowth in front of the Confederate works.

When the Confederates saw that many of the advancing Federal troops were black they became enraged. Lieutenant John Web, his brother Thomas, and several others of the 8th Tennessee Cavalry jumped from behind the Confederate breastworks and attacked the blacks with their pistols. The men of the 5th USCC killed John Web and wounded the others.

As the Federals advanced they found a gap in the line between Confederate General Felix H. Robertson's Brigade on the left and some of the reserves on the right. Robertson withdrew his brigade without warning and left Colonel George G. Dibrell's Brigade almost surrounded, and a large gap in the center of the Confederate line. The Federal attackers took full advantage of the opportunity and pressed the Confederates to the top of the ridge. Armed with Spencer repeating carbines, the men of the 11th Michigan Cavalry and 12th Ohio Cavalry had an advantage over Robertson's and Dibrell's men. Yet as the day progressed the men in Ratliff's Brigade began to run low on ammunition.

Many were impressed by the performance of the blacks in the charge. An officer of the 13th Kentucky Cavalry admitted that he "never thought they would fight until he saw them there." He added that he "never saw troops fight like they did. The Rebels were firing on them with grape and canister and were mowing them down by the scores but others kept straight on." Leading the blacks as they took the Confederate works, Colonel Brisbin noted: "I have seen white troops fight in twenty-seven battles and I never saw any fight better."

Several of the young boys in Colonel Robert Preston's

Southern militia had been "sighting their guns and showing how they would shoot a nigger, if they had a chance." The breach in the left of the line gave the boys their opportunity. Half of Preston's reserves went across the road and up to Chestnut Ridge. The militia fought with Ratliff's Brigade for fifteen minutes until the Confederate line stabilized and the immediate crisis passed. The militia then returned to its place as a reserve with the loss of one or two men.

The Federals soon launched an attack on the Confederate center. General Edward H. Hobson's Brigade made the advance from three angles, all converging upon Colonel Edwin Trimble's 10th Kentucky Cavalry at the ford. One column advanced down Sanders's Hill, a second followed the river, and a third moved across Broady Bottom. Union troops drove Giltner from the ford as he attempted to consolidate his brigade.

As the Southerners fell back, artillery at the church helped

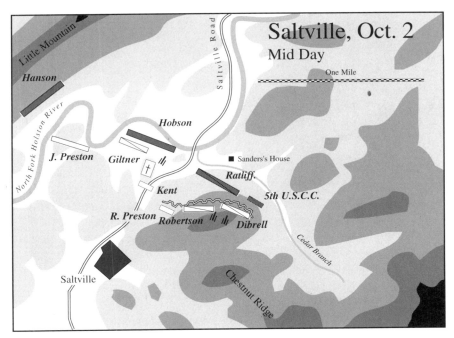

compensate for their lack of numbers. The Confederates watched as "one shot killed a major and a captain. At another time a few well-directed shots stampeded a Federal line advancing around the end of Chestnut Ridge."

Forced back from the river, the Confederates attempted to

Edward H. Hobson: born Kentucky 1825; he was educated in local schools near his home in Greensburg, Kentucky; as a young man he when into business with his father, a steamboat operator and merchant; the younger Hobson fought in the Mexican War, earning promotion to 1st lieutenant for his actions at Buena Vista; returning to Kentucky he became a successful merchant and banker; following the outbreak of the Civil War, Hobson recruited a regiment that became the 13th

Kentucky (US) Infantry and was commissioned its colonel in January 1862; after leading his regiment at Shiloh in April 1862, he spent the balance of the war operating in and around his native Kentucky; promoted to brigadier general of volunteers in April 1863, Hobson headed a brigade in the pursuit of Rebel General John Hunt Morgan's July 1863 Ohio Raid; at Buffington's Island on the Ohio River Hobson's force shared in the defeat of Morgan and the capture of a large number of Confederate raiders; days later Hobson's Brigade captured Morgan himself near New Lisbon; ironically, Morgan, who escaped from an Ohio prison, returned to Kentucky less than a year later and captured Hobson and his entire command at Cynthiana; Hobson drew censure for an unorthodox parole agreement reached with his captor, in which he would go, under escort, to Ohio and personally lobby for the exchange of Confederate prisoners; the deal fell through, however, and Morgan was killed shortly thereafter; this episode may have cost Hobson a brevet he should have garnered for his earlier efforts; in October 1864 he led a mounted brigade in General Stephen Burbridge's repulse at Saltville, Virginia; thereafter he commanded the First Division, District of Kentucky, at Lexington until mustered out in August 1865; after the war he was active in Radical Republican politics and the Grand Army of the Republic. General Hobson died at a Grand Army of the Republic reunion encampment at Cleveland, Ohio, in 1901.

hold a line in a clearing in front of the log church. Heavily out-numbered, Giltner galloped back to the church and ordered up a battalion of reserves to help Trimble's 10th Kentucky Cavalry. Two companies under Captain Peter Gallagher from Joseph F. Kent's militia battalion responded. The reserves charged up to the graveyard and joined Trimble's line. They advanced within fifty feet of the Federals, fired one volley, then fell back to the church in confusion, leaving fourteen dead and wounded on the field. Their disorganized attack and retreat caused even more chaos in the Confederate line.

As Colonel Trimble attempted to rally his men, he suddenly "sprang up high in the air, with arms and legs extended full length. He leaped at least five feet, and fell to the ground col-lapsed and stone dead." Trimble had been hit in the head with the ball entering just below a star on his hat. His 10th Kentucky Cavalry lost almost all of its officers in the fight and fell back in confusion to the protection of the battery at the church. The Federals did not follow.

During the attack at the ford, the sound of gunfire in the rear of the Federal army surprised men on both sides. It was from a detached company of Confederates under Captain Bart Jenkins, who had been separated from Giltner's Brigade earli-er. Although he had been out of communication with Giltner for two days, Jenkins with a company of local militia had stayed with the Federal army and took the opportunity to attack Burbridge's unguarded horses and pack train. The diver-sion drew off five hundred Federals from the attack at the ford. Burbridge repulsed the attack, but it gave him the impression that he was totally surrounded.

The two Federal assaults now stalled. While Ratliff's Brigade maintained a tenuous hold on part of the line on Chestnut Ridge, Hobson's advance came to a standstill in front of the church. On the Confederate left, the Federals made one final assault.

Throughout the day Southerners had watched as Federal

Colonel Charles Hanson's Brigade dismounted and marched up the face of Little Mountain. Hanson planned to take the Confederates left flank; yet as his command emerged from the woods, the Federals found Southerners posted at the top of a steep cliff on the far side of the Holston River. They were the 4th Kentucky Cavalry and Colonel James T. Preston's Battalion of local reserves.

The Kentucky troopers discarded the idea of carrying short cavalry muskets and met the Federals with long-range Enfield rifles. As the 4th took aim on the attackers attempting to cross the river, the men challenged the Yankees to "come right up and draw your salt." One Kentucky trooper, Silas Sims, had a reputation as an excellent marksman. He would fire and yell: "Yank, How's that? Am I shooting too high or too low?"

This final attack failed to dislodge the Confederates and cost the Federals over one hundred casualties, including Colonel Hanson. Shot in the abdomen, Hanson passed command to the

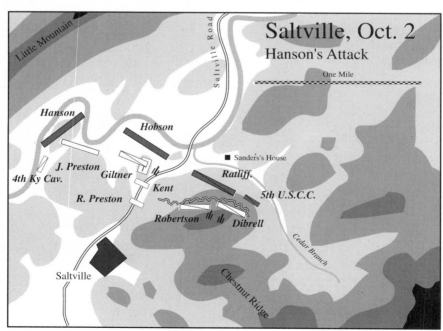

colonel of the 40th Kentucky, who was half a mile in the rear with the reserves. The brigade then fell back in disorder.

The Southern lines at Saltville had held off all assults and at about 5 P.M. Burbridge decided to retreat. Ratliff's cavalry, including the black troops, held the Confederate works until dark. At nightfall the Federals, exhausted and out of ammunition, pulled back from their advanced position, building large

Basil Wilson Duke: born Kentucky 1838; son of a naval officer; educated at Centre College and the Transylvania University Law School; was practicing law in St. Louis during the secession crisis; appointed by the governor to the city's police commission and sent south to secure cannon for the secessionist militia; returned to Kentucky and married Henrietta Hunt Morgan, sister of the Confederate cavalry raider John Hunt Morgan; in 1861 enlisted as a private in the Lexington Rifles, his brother-in-law's company, which soon elected him 2d lieutenant; when this company became part of the 2d Kentucky Cavalry, Duke was appointed lieutenant colonel and later colonel; one of his men called him "the coolest and always most self-possessed officer that we encountered during the war"; conspicuous during the operations of Morgan's command, Duke was captured during the celebrated raid into Ohio and Indiana and was a prisoner of war for more than a year; after his exchange, he commanded in Eastern Kentucky and Western Virginia, and was promoted to brigadier general in 1864; in the closing days of the war, his brigade escorted Jefferson Davis and the fugitive Confederate government; following the war, General Duke had a distinguished career as lawyer, legislator, author, and editor. He wrote his own *Reminiscences* (1911) and *History of Morgan's Cavalry* (1906); he edited *Southern Bivouac*, a Confederate veterans' magazine, and he was commissioner of Shiloh National Military Park from 1895 until his death in New York City in 1916. An enlisted man wrote: "I never saw a more graceful figure on horseback, erect and handsome…stately, elegantly attired. He was the impersonation of the ideal cavalier, a veritable Prince Rupert, or Henry of Navarre…an attractive, martial figure."

fires in order to deceive the Confederates into thinking that they would remain. They left most of their dead and wounded on the field.

Following Burbridge's withdrawal, some Confederates advanced into the vacant Union position. Silas Sims, the marksman of the 4th Kentucky Cavalry, found a dead Federal officer who had been hit in the head by an artillery shell. Sims reached into his haversack, brought forth a handful of salt and poured it into the open skull. "There," he said to the corpse, "you came for some salt, now take some."

As the battle ended, Confederate Generals John C. Breckinridge and John Echols arrived from Abingdon, where they had been coordinating the concentration of troops. Other rein-

Felix H. Robertson: born Texas 1839; son of General Jerome B. Robertson; attended Baylor University; appointed to West Point in 1857, but resigned on January 29, 1861, to offer his services to the Confederacy; commissioned 2d lieu-

tenant of artillery, he took part in the reduction of Fort Sumter, then served at Pensacola on the staff of General Adley Gladden; at Shiloh, he commanded a battery with the rank of captain; accompanied General Braxton Bragg's Kentucky Campaign, but saw no action at Perryville; fought at Murfreesboro, but following the battle, Robertson joined the dispute between General Bragg and General John C. Breckinridge; according to Breckinridge's biography, Robertson submitted a perjured report detrimental to Breckinridge; promoted to major after Murfreesboro, he led a battalion in General James Longstreet's Corps at Chickamauga; in January 1864 promoted to lieutenant colonel and given command of the artillery of General Joseph Wheeler's Cavalry Corps, with which he served during the Atlanta Campaign; in July 1864 President Davis appointed Robertson a brigadier general; after raiding around Atlanta, he took a small brigade of Wheeler's cavalry and, assisted by General John S. Williams, rode to blunt a forcements streamed in as well, including the cavalry brigades of Generals Basil Duke, George Cosby, and John Vaughn.

After dark, Captain Edward O. Guerrant and his aide, Trooper George Dallas Mosgrove of the 4th Kentucky Cavalry, met with General Felix Robertson. Mosgrove noted that Robertson "was the youngest looking General in the army, apparently not more than twenty-four years of age...." During the meeting the "gallant and handsome" Robertson proudly informed Guerrant that "he had killed nearly all the negroes." Evidently, Robertson and the Confederats saw no reason to take any black prisoners during the battle. A member of the 4th Kentucky Cavalry later remembered "we surely slew negroes that day."

Federal raid on Saltville, Virginia, where Robertson and his men broke the attack; but the next day "his men began the systematic execution of the blacks, and not a few of their wounded white brethren"; General Breckinridge arrived and reported the incident to General Lee, who ordered that Robertson be arrested and brought to trial, but Robertson quickly left Breckinridge's jurisdiction; in action again at Buckhead Creek, near Waynesborough, Georgia, in November 1864, Robertson "again showed the ugly side of his nature"; a trooper tried to stop some fellow Confederates from shooting four captured Yankees, when Robertson rode up and said: "They know best what to do with them." The prisoners were shot, and Robertson himself soon fell with a severe wound; he saw no further active service, but in April 1865 was sent by General Howell Cobb to treat for the surrender of the city of Macon with his old West Point associate, Union Major General James H. Wilson; in February 1865 the Confederate Senate refused to confirm Robertson at any grade from major to brigadier; after the war, he returned to Texas, settling in Waco to practice law; at the time of his death there, in 1928, he had been for many years dean of the local bar. A soldier, who was at Saltville, wrote: "I was charmed with the appearance of General Robertson. He was the youngest looking general I had seen in the army, ...and wearing good clothes, en negligee, gallant and hand-some." But his biographer sees Robertson as "perjurer, sycophant, quite probably a murderer, [and] almost without doubt the most reprehensible man in either army to wear the uniform of a general. Only by the narrowest of margins did he escape being tried by his own government for what later generations would call war crimes."

The black troops knew what was coming for they were aware that some of the men the Confederates captured during the battle had already been murdered. As Burbridge began his retreat, many seriously wounded black soldiers attempted to follow. Colonel Brisbin looked on in horror as he "saw one man riding with his arm off, another shot through the lungs, and another shot through both hips," all attempting to evade the Confederates. Later he reported shocking casualty figures that included at least 118 of the four hundred men of the 5th USCC who took part in the fight were killed, wounded, or missing.

The Southerners had saved the saltworks. They had put up a stout defense with men emptying their cartridge boxes as many as three times. Some had fired over one hundred rounds each. With the timely arrival of reinforcements and the unexpected gallantry of the reserves, the Confederates had won the battle of Saltville. While the battle had ended, the killing had just begun.

4
"Our Men Took No Negro Prisoners"

In the early morning fog on October 3 Confederate Trooper George Mosgrove heard firing along the line. Thinking it meant a new Federal attack, he noted: "Presently I heard a shot, then another and another until the firing swelled to the volume of a skirmish line." He then mounted his horse and rode forward to ascertain the·source of the shooting. Arriving in front of Dibrell's and Robertson's Brigades on Chestnut Ridge, he "found the Tennesseans were killing negroes…. Hearing more firing at the front, I cautiously rode forward and came upon a squad of Tennesseans, mad and excited to the highest degree. They were shooting every wounded negro they could find. Hearing firing on other parts of the field, I knew the same awful work was going on all about me."

Mosgrove was appalled, yet he admitted that it would have

been futile (if not dangerous) to attempt to stop it. He added: "Some were so slightly wounded that they could run, but when they ran from the muzzle of one pistol it was only to be confronted by another."

Confederate Captain Edwin O. Guerrant also heard the firing and noted in his diary that day, "scouts were sent [and] went all over the field and the continual sing of the rifle, sung the death knell of many a poor negro who was unfortunate enough not to be killed yesterday. Our men took no negro prisoners. Great numbers of them were killed yesterday and today."

Private Harry Shocker, a wounded prisoner from the 12th Ohio Cavalry, also witnessed the carnage. He watched in horror as a Confederate guerrilla, the notorious Champ Ferguson, calmly walked about the battlefield killing white prisoners as well as blacks. Shocker looked on as he "saw him pointing his

Champ Ferguson: born Kentucky 1821; he received little formal education in Clinton County, a mountainous area along the Kentucky-Tennessee border; people of the Cumberland Mountain region were bitterly divided over the question of secession and the coming of the Civil War rendered the area a hotbed of partisan activity, in which personal as well as political differences were prosecuted; few of the partisans belonged to organized regiments or regular units; in this environment Ferguson became a prominent player; already a troublemaker before the war, in 1862 Ferguson organized a partisan company based in the pro-Confederate area around Sparta, Tennessee; Ferguson and as many as sixty followers routinely raided into Kentucky and harassed Federal forces that operated in the region; frequently, Ferguson's and other bands served regular units as guides; in August 1864 Ferguson and some of his men joined General Joseph Wheeler's force when the young

pistol down at prisoners lying on the ground, and heard the reports of the pistol and the screams of the men." Shocker crawled off and hid as Ferguson approached one of his comrades, a wounded friend from the 12th Ohio, Crawford Hazlewood, and asked him "why he came up there to fight with the damn niggers?" He then asked Hazlewood, "Where will you have it, in the back or the face?" The man pleaded for his life, but as Shocker watched helplessly, Ferguson killed Hazlewood too. Shocker later saw Ferguson kill four black men at a cabin on Sanders's land.

Sanders's house had been the center of Ratliff's Union line. Many of the men who had been wounded in the charge were brought to the farm and left during the retreat. Mosgrove found seven or eight slightly wounded blacks in a cabin. The men were lined up with their backs against the walls. As Mosgrove stepped in, "a pistol-shot from the door caused me to turn and

cavalry commander raided into eastern Tennessee; Ferguson remained with Wheeler for a time riding as far as Georgia before returning to support General John C. Breckenridge in southwestern Virginia; following the October 1864 Battle of Saltville, Ferguson played a major role in the massacre of dozens of wounded black prisoners and white officers, including Lieutenant Elza Smith; Ferguson briefly rejoined Wheeler's cavalry, but became unruly under military command and was arrested; Richmond authorities ordered Ferguson sent back to Virginia to stand trial in early 1865, but he was soon paroled as Confederate prosecutors lacked the witnesses to gain a conviction; the Federals, however, retained a keen interest; after Ferguson's surrender was rejected, he was treated as an outlaw; he was captured in May 1865 and imprisoned, Nashville pending trial; a military court found Ferguson guilty of 53 murders; the trial, focusing predominantly on the killing of Lieutenant Smith, made little mention of the countless black troopers slain; Champ Ferguson was hanged on October 20, 1865. A wartime story maintains that Ferguson began fighting in response to abuses committed on his wife and daughter by eleven Federal raiders early in the war and that among these was Elza Smith. The story further asserts that Ferguson then raised his partisan company and pledged publicly not to rest until he had killed all eleven offenders. Ferguson stands with Andersonville prison commandant Henry Wirz as the only Confederates executed for war crimes.

observe a boy, not more than sixteen years old, with a pistol in each hand." Mosgrove told the boy to hold his fire while he jumped out of the way. He then added, "in less time than I can write it, the boy had shot every negro in the room."

Captain Orange Sells of the 12th Ohio Cavalry was also at the cabin. He saw "a good many negroes killed there. All of them were soldiers and all were wounded but one. I heard firing there all over the place; it was like a skirmish."

Lieutenant George W. Carter of the 11th Michigan Cavalry looked on as eight or nine blacks were killed: "I couldn't tell whether or not citizens or soldiers did the killing of the prisoners, as all seemed to be dressed alike." While many Confederates were local civilians called up as reserves, the veteran Confederate regiments were also known for their non-military appearance.

Later that morning Mosgrove watched as General Breckinridge, General Duke, and other officers rode to the front. The scene infuriated Breckinridge. "With blazing eyes and thunderous tones, [he] ordered that the massacre should be stopped. He rode away and–the shooting went on. The men could not be restrained." Mosgrove asserted that he did not see any Kentuckians of his unit involved in the murders, although he admitted that they could have been. He blamed the slaughter on the Tennessee brigades of Felix H. Robertson and George D. Dibrell.

Later Mosgrove saw a black boy "who seemed to think he was in no danger." A young Confederate approached him and drew his pistol, "and then the little mulatto jumped behind a sapling not larger than a man's arm, and cried out that General Duke had ordered him to remain there until he should return. It was no use. In another moment the little mulatto was a corpse."

After attempting to stop the massacre, Breckinridge organized a pursuit of the Federals. He ordered Giltner's Brigade to prepare to follow them, then directed Williams to take his brigade and those of Duke, Cosby, Vaughn, Dibrell, and Robertson along a parallel route to Hayter's Gap in order to cut off the Federal retreat.

As Burbridge continued his retreat, a courier met the column; bringing the orders from General Sherman directing him to cancel the raid and proceed with his full force to Knoxville to protect Sherman's supply line against Forrest's attacks. Burbridge and General McLean left the column and headed for Lexington. The Federal force then outran its pursuers and safely made it back to Kentucky.

5

"ONE OF THE MOST DIABOLICAL ACTS OF THE WAR"

On October 3 word reached Richmond of the Confederate victory. General Echols wrote the commander of the reserve forces in Virginia, General James L. Kemper, to commend him on the fine performance of his militia. He added, "there were two or three regiments of negro troops, which were badly cut up." On October 4 General Robert E. Lee issued an official report on the battle to Confederate Secretary of War James A. Seddon. He informed Seddon that the "enemy attacked Saltville on the 2nd instant and received a bloody repulse. They retired during the night in confusion...leaving most of their dead and wounded on our hands.... All our troops behaved well." Yet as time passed the truth about the battle reached Richmond as the murders continued around Saltville.

The Confederates gathered many of the remaining wounded

Federals and moved them to nearby Emory and Henry College, which had been converted into an army hospital. After the battle it served both the Federal and Confederate wounded. Federal Surgeon William H. Gardner of the 30th Kentucky Infantry treated many of the casualties at Emory and Henry. At 10 P.M. on October 7 Gardner saw several men force their way past the Confederate staff at the hospital and murder two blacks in their beds. The next day the Southerners sent sixty-one wounded prisoners from the hospital to Lynchburg. Many others were too severely wounded to travel, and each day the Confederates brought in more captives.

At 4 P.M. on October 8 several men in Confederate uniform forced their way past the hospital guards. Many people recognized the guerrilla Champ Ferguson as the leader of the band. Wounded Union trooper Harry Shocker again found his life threatened by the guerrilla chief. Ferguson approached Shocker and asked him if he knew Lieutenant Elza C. Smith of the 13th Kentucky Cavalry. He added: "I have a grudge against Smith: we'll find him." Smith and Ferguson were friends (perhaps related to each other) in Kentucky prior to the conflict, and with the war their earlier relationship had developed into a no-quarter guerrilla fight.

Leaving Shocker, Ferguson eventually found Smith's bed. Looking up, Smith asked: "Champ is that you?" Ferguson lowered his gun and replied, "Smith, do you see this?" He then leveled the weapon at Smith's head and attempted to fire. The cap failed to ignite the charge, and Ferguson had to cock and pull the trigger two more times before it went off, killing Smith.

Ferguson then set out to murder Colonel Charles Hanson of the 13th Kentucky Cavalry, as well as a captain from the 12th Ohio Cavalry. Before he could accomplish this, however, the Confederate hospital staff—at the risk of their own lives—intervened and dissuaded Ferguson. The next day the Confederates defused the situation by moving the rest of the wounded prisoners to Lynchburg. Meanwhile Ferguson left the department.

Emory and Henry College, ca. 1874

By the end of the week the Richmond papers were proclaiming a great victory in southwest Virginia over Burbridge and his army. The Richmond *Enquirer* proudly ran a segregated casualty list:

Killed, (Yankee Whites)	106
Negroes,	150
Wounded, (Whites)	80
Negroes,	6

Evidently the *Enquirer* did not feel the need to explain the disparity in numbers between the wounded whites and blacks.

The Richmond *Dispatch* joined in with a gloating editorial: "They routed Burbridge and all his 'niggers,' horse, foot and dragoon. Abundant as the article was in that region, they could not put a grain of salt on the tails of the flying black birds." The article reached a peak as the editor concluded: "The country has since been infested with birds of the same color, but greater respectability. They are turkey-buzzards this time, and they come in quest of Yankee carcasses."

Following his parole and return to Federal lines, Surgeon Gardner filed a report on the massacre. General McLean endorsed it with a demand that the murderers be delivered to Union authorities for punishment. "In case of refusal [he urged] that immediate retaliation be enforced upon such Confederate prisoners as we may have in our possession, man for man." On October 18 the Federals delivered Gardner's report to Lee's headquarters by a truce boat.

Breckinridge had already informed Lee of the murders, and he accused Texas General Felix H. Robertson of directing the killings. On October 21 Lee's aide-de-camp reported to Breckinridge that the general was "much pained to hear of the treatment the negro prisoners are reported to have received, and agrees with you in entirely condemning it. That a general officer should have been guilty of the crime you mention meets with his unqualified reprobation. He directs that if the officer is still in your department you should prefer charges against him and bring him to trial."

Yet Robertson slipped away from Breckinridge's court of inquiry and left the department to join General Joseph Wheeler's cavalry in Georgia. After his departure, his brigade became completely insubordinate, the men refused to obey orders and terrorized all communities they passed through. Roberson was never charged by the Confederates, probably because the final events of the war overshadowed his actions.

As the Federal force made its disorganized retreat to Kentucky, the 5th USCC reported losing 118 of its 400 men. Yet the regiment had not even been organized prior to the battle. The lack of organization of the regiment at the time makes it difficult to determine exactly how many men were murdered at Saltville. Few officers and noncommissioned officers were at their posts, and one black sergeant later admitted that he did not even know the names of his men at the time of the battle. On October 30th the 5th USCC was finally organized as a regiment.

As the Federals reorganized in Kentucky, many of the men originally listed as missing in action from the 5th drifted into camp. A few of them had deserted during the campaign. Samuel Harrison of Company G had been listed as missing in action after the battle, but he later returned to the unit and was court martialed for desertion. Alex Young of Company L returned to the regiment in April 1865; a court martial sentenced him to one year at hard labor for deserting at Saltville.

The men of the 5th USCC had little doubt as to the fate of their missing comrades. Colonel Wade noted in October 1864 that his men "participated in a very severe engagement losing a large number of killed and wounded and missing; those who fell into the hands of the enemy were supposed to have been murdered." Lieutenant Augustus Flint of Company E reported that the twelve men missing from his company were massacred by the Confederates. The commander of Company C noted that he had left eight wounded men on the field at Saltville and was unsure of their fate. White troops also attempted to make sense of the events after the battle. The historian of the 12th Ohio Cavalry recorded that Jacob. C. Pence had been listed as missing at Saltville and that he was "supposed to have been killed by Champ Ferguson."

In Kentucky, General Burbridge made efforts to apprehend Ferguson. Under a flag of truce Burbridge informed Confederate General Duke that he considered the murder of Lieutenant Smith "one of the most diabolical acts of the war." He also warned that if the Federals captured Ferguson and his band "they would not be treated as prisoners."

Although the Confederates had no desire to turn Ferguson over to the U.S. Army, Breckinridge had no intention of letting him get away with murder. Upon hearing of the killings, he had ordered Ferguson's arrest. Although Ferguson had slipped out of the department, by February 5, 1865, the Confederates had captured and imprisoned the guerrilla in Wytheville, Virginia, but by the end of the month he had been released on parole. Although the exact reason for Ferguson's release is unclear, it is likely that the Confederates could not find any witnesses to testify against him. Many of the troops who had seen the massacre were out of the department; others obviously condoned his actions by their own participation in the killings. The witnesses were also aware that Ferguson led a gang of killers. Since the Confederate government was no longer able to enforce law and order, it is doubtful that they could have safely testified against him. Finally, the Confederate government was rapidly collapsing. As with Robertson, the approaching end of the war may have overshadowed Southern efforts to convict Ferguson.

6
CONCLUSION

The Federals soon returned to southwest Virginia, for the area had vital resources that Union authorities could not ignore. In December 1864 General George Stoneman, the new commander of the Department of the Ohio, launched his own raid into Virginia. Stoneman's plan was to return to southwest Virginia with Burbridge and remove Breckinridge as a threat.

The Union raiders again picked up the 5th USCC as well as the newly created 6th USCC. The survivors of the massacre were more than ready to avenge Saltville. On December 17-18, outnumbering the Confederates four to one, the Federals took on Breckinridge along the Holston River about a mile outside Marion, Virginia. After two days of indecisive action, Breckinridge withdrew with his command.

After Breckinridge retreated the Federals were finally free to take the resources of southwest Virginia. On December 20 Stoneman captured Saltville and began destroying the works.

He also did considerable damage to the lead mines, the Virginia and Tennessee Railroad, and the towns of Abingdon, Wytheville, and Bristol. While the damage to the railroad and saltworks could be repaired, the government stores destroyed in the towns could not be replaced.

The black troops performed admirably in Marion and continued to add to their hard-won reputation. Even former enemies praised their performance. They had won their spurs and would remain on active duty for almost a year after Appomattox. On March 16, 1866, the 5th United States Colored Cavalry held its final formation in Helena, Arkansas. The horsemen had paid the full price for their freedom.

On February 18, 1865, Federal authorities relieved Burbridge of command. Most likely his demise was caused by his controversial handling of civilian affairs in Kentucky and

George Stoneman: born New York 1822; graduated from the U.S. Military Academy in 1846, thirty-third in his class of fifty-nine that included "Stonewall"

Jackson, George B. McClellan, George Pickett, and several other future Civil War generals; posted to dragoons and commissioned 2d lieutenant, he served in California during the Mexican War; promoted to 1st lieutenant, his service was largely in the Southwest; in 1855 he became a captain in the newly-formed elite 2d Cavalry in Texas; he managed to escape capture following the surrender of Texas' military facilities in 1861; promoted to major in the 1st (later 4th) U.S. Cavalry at the outbreak of the Civil War; commissioned brigadier general of volunteers in August 1861; he held a variety of cavalry commands in the Army of the Potomac in the early stages of the war, including a division during the Peninsular Campaign; he led an infantry division at Antietam in September 1862; promoted to major general of volunteers in November, he led a corps at Fredericksburg in December; he then commanded the Cavalry Corps, Army of the Potomac, but his

his botched raid on Saltville. He was despised by Federals as well as Confederates; both sides were delighted to see his rule come to an end.

As for the murderers, Champ Ferguson became the only person ever brought to justice for the massacre at Saltville. After Appomattox, the Federals captured Ferguson and on May 25 put him on trial at Nashville, Tennessee. They charged him with the murder of Lieutenant Elza Smith as well as "twelve soldiers whose names are unknown at Saltville, Virginia," and "two negro soldiers, names unknown, while lying wounded in prison, at Saltville." In total, the court found Ferguson guilty of murdering fifty-three men and convicted him as a "border rebel guerrilla, robber and murderer."

On October 20, 1865, Ferguson was hanged. Standing silently nearby as witnesses to the execution were the men of

ill-timed and ineffectual raid during the Chancellorsville Campaign in May 1863 left General Joseph Hooker's force open to surprise and defeat; although not at fault, Stoneman was relieved; he then headed the Cavalry Bureau in Washington, D.C., for the remainder of the year; transferred to the Western Theater in January 1864, he commanded briefly the Twenty-third Corps, Army of the Ohio, before assuming direction of that army's cavalry division; he led his division in the Atlanta Campaign but was captured with a large portion of his command during a ill-conceived and poorly executed raid in July 1864; exchanged in October, he took command of the Department of the Ohio and in December led a month-long raid on the salt works and lead mines in southwestern Virginia; in March 1865 he assumed direction of the District of East Tennessee from which he led a highly effective raid into North Carolina in support of General W.T. Sherman's campaign in that state; brevetted through major general in the regular army, he mustered out of the volunteer organization and reverted to his actual rank of lieutenant colonel (since 1863); in the post-war reorganization of the army he became colonel of the 21st Infantry, serving mostly in Arizona until resigning his commission in 1871; settling on his estate near Los Angeles, he served as railroad commissioner and as Democratic governor of California from 1883 to 1887. General Stoneman died at Buffalo, New York, in 1894. He was among the Union's most experienced cavalry officers. Despite his miserable performance in the Atlanta Campaign, Stoneman was essentially a capable soldier.

the 15th United States Colored Infantry, whose presence added an element of poetic justice to the end of Ferguson's brutal life.

Arriving in Georgia after Saltville, General Felix Robertson was severely wounded near Augusta at Buckhead Creek at the end of November 1864. Robertson never returned to duty, and avoided any inquiry of the massacre. Yet the Confederate Congress withheld confirmation of his promotion to general. This may have been directly caused by his actions at Saltville. Later he returned to his home in Texas and began a profitable law career in Waco. Robertson died in 1928; ironically, he was to be the last Confederate general to perish.

A conservative estimate of the number of blacks murdered at Saltville is forty-six. These are the men listed and kept on the rolls as M.I.A.'s until well after the war. Not only does Saltville stand as possibly the worst battlefield atrocity of the Civil War, it also demonstrates one of the factors that cause the "rules of war" to break down. In warfare, as religion, race, and culture conflict on the battlefield, the chance for a massacre of prisoners increases.

From Powhatan's War at Jamestown to Wounded Knee in 1890, Native Americans and European descendents often killed their prisoners. The Indian Wars became a struggle for religious and racial survival, and the victors repeatedly felt justified in slaughtering their prisoners. The goal of this type of fighting went beyond that of victory; it included racial survival.

The massacre at Saltville was not an isolated incident. At Saltville, men on both sides were aware of the fate of the blacks at Fort Pillow. To the Confederates, the sight of armed black men was their worst nightmare. Raised on stories of Nat Turner's rebellion and the recent memory of John Brown, Southerners felt that the presence of blacks on the battlefield raised the stakes from that of a civil war of independence to that of a total war over race. Neither side could expect quarter.

Note: Portions of The Table of Organization presented in Appendices A and B are taken from William Marvel, "The Battle of Saltville: Massacre or Myth?" *Blue & Gray Magazine*, Vol. 8. No. 6, Aug. 1991.

APPENDIX A

ORGANIZATION AND CASUALTIES OF FEDERAL FORCES

COMMANDER

GEN. STEPHEN G. BURBRIDGE
GEN. NATHANIEL C. MCLEAN'S KENTUCKY DIVISION
BRIG. GEN. EDWARD H. HOBSON'S BRIGADE

	KIA	WIA	MIA
13th Kentucky Cav.	4	13	1
30th Kentucky Mtd. Inf.	5	2	—
35th Kentucky Mtd. Inf.	3	11	21
40th Kentucky Mtd. Inf.	—	1	—
45th Kentucky Mtd. Inf.	—	2	—

COL. CHARLES HANSON'S BRIGADE

	KIA	WIA	MIA
11th Kentucky Cav.	—	10	1
26th Kentucky Mtd. Inf.	1	3	—
37th Kentucky Mtd. Inf.	2	9	—
39th Kentucky Mtd. Inf.	1	10	—

COL. ROBERT RATLIFF'S BRIGADE

	KIA	WIA	MIA
5th United States Colored Cav. (with two companies from the 6th USCC)	10	37	46*
11th Michigan Cav.	11	61	16
12th Ohio Cav.	5	31	12

Six mountain howitzers,
Lt. Wallace of 40th Kentucky Mtd. Inf.   —   —   —

Federal Totals: 42   190   97

* This number represents the number of men massacred after the battle.

APPENDIX B

ORGANIZATION AND CASUALTIES
OF CONFEDERATE FORCES
COMMANDERS

BRIG. GEN. JOHN S. WILLIAMS AIDED BY BRIG. GEN. ALFRED E. JACKSON.
ARRIVING LATE IN THE DAY WERE
MAJ. GEN. JOHN C. BRECKINRIDGE AND BRIG. GEN. JOHN ECHOLS.

COL. HENRY L. GILTNER'S BRIGADE

	KIA	WIA	MIA
4th Kentucky Cavalry	—	—	—
10th Kentucky Cavalry	—	—	—
10th Kentucky Mtd. R.	—	—	—
64th Virginia Mtd. Inf.	—	—	—
Capt. Barton W. Jenkins			
Co. of Kentucky Cav.	—	—	—

BRIG. GEN. JOHN S. WILLIAMS
CAVALRY DIVISION

COL. WILLIAM C.P. BRECKINRIDGE'S BRIGADE

	KIA	WIA	MIA
1st Kentucky Cav.	—	—	—
9th Kentucky Cav.	—	—	—

COL. GEORGE G. DIBRELL'S BRIGADE

4th Tennessee Cav.	—	—	—
8th Tennessee Cav.	—	—	—
9th Tennessee Cav.	—	—	—

BRIG. GEN. FELIX H. ROBERTSON'S BRIGADE

3rd Confederate Cav. (partial)	—	—	—
6th Confederate Cav. (partial)	—	—	—
8th Confederate Cav. (one btn.)	—	—	—
10th Confederate Cav.	—	—	—
5th Georgia Cav. (partial)	—	—	—

RESERVES
COL. ROBERT H. SMITHS BTN.

Smyth, Russell, Tazewell, Washington	13	51	21

COL. ROBERT T. PRESTON'S BTN

Montgomery	2	5	—

COL. KENTS BTN.Wythe

Carroll, Grayson	3	18	1

COL. JAMES PRESTON'S BTN

Saltville area	—	—	—

ARTILLERY
CAPT. HUGH L.W. McCLUNG'S

Tennessee battery	—	—	—

CAPT. JOHN W. BARR'S

Virginia battery	—	—	—
Confederate total (estimate):	30	100	30

APPENDIX C

MEN LISTED AS MISSING IN ACTION
FROM THE 5TH AND 6TH USCC, 1864-1865.

Anderson, Jefferson	Co. M.
Bailey, Walker	Co. E.
Baker, William	Co. E.
Black, Joseph	Co. B.
Brown, Jefferson	Co. E.
Cissell, Charles	Co. C.
Brown, Lewis	Co. C.
Cissell, Edward	Co. C.
Cissell, William	Co. C.
Clay, John	Co. B.
Coleman, Allen	Co. E.
Crutcher, Andrew	Co. B.
Drain, John	Co. H.
Dunn, William	Co. M.
Dunston, Noah	Co. B.
Farris, Aaron	Co. B. (6th USCC)
Finch, Peter	Co. H.
Flernoy, Joseph	Co. H.
Ford, Frank	Co. E.
Fox, Wiley	Co. H.
Garry, William	Co. H.
Gordon, Philip	Co. H.
Grey, Anderson	Co. E.
Grigsby, George	Co. M.
Grigsby, Richard	Co. M.
Hackley, James	Co. E.
Harris, Samuel	Co. E.
Harrison, Henry	Co. E.
Harrison, Solomon	Co. B.
Hicks, David	Co. B.

Hunter, John	Co. M.
Jackson, Moses	Co. H.
Jackson, Thomas	Co. M.
James, James	Co. M.
Johnson, Ellis	Co. B. (6th USCC)
Johnston, Benjamin	Co. M.
Jones, Lewis	Co. E.
Lampkins, Harrison	Co. E.
Lewis, Benjamin	Co. E.
Lewis, George	Co. B.
Lewis, James	Co. B. (6th USCC)
Lirch, Julius	Co. B.
Martin, William	Co. E.
Martin, Zachariah	Co. M.
Mason, Robert	Co. M.
Massey, Joseph	Co. M.
McCall, Marcellus	Co. E.
Miller, Sam	Co. C.
Mitchell, Henry	Co. C.
Moton, Jerry	Co. E.
Moton, Lewis	Co. E.
Moton, Samuel	Co. E.
Murthey, Moton	Co. E.
Parish, David	Co. E.
Phelps, Shelby	Co. E.
Roberts, Benjamin	Co. C.
Scott, King	Co. M.
Scott, Lowrie	Co. M.
Seals, Alexander	Co. E.
Simpson, Isaiah	Co. M.
Sloan, Thomas	Co. E.
Smithson, James	Co. E.
Thomas, Grant	Co. E.
Thompson, Albert	Co. E.
Tutt, Peter	Co. C.
White, George	Co. E.

Killed in Action 1864–1865.

Clay, James	Co. M.
Harlitt, James	Co. I.
Pruit, Andrew	Co. A. (6th USCC)
Pruit, John	Co. A. (6th USCC)
Walker, Gabriel	Co. D.
Weeks, George	Co. D.

FURTHER READING

Boatner, Mark M. III, *The Civil War Dictionary.* New York: 1987.

Brock, R. A. *Hardesty's Historical and Geographical Encyclopedia...Special Virginia Addition.* Richmond: 1884.

Bruce, Thomas *Southwest Virginia and the Valley: Historical and Biographical.* Roanoke, Va: 1892.

Castle, Robert. "The Fort Pillow Massacre: A Fresh Examination of the Evidence." *Civil War History,* March 1958, 37–50.

Cimprich, John and Mainfort, Robert C. "Fort Pillow Revisited: New Evidence about an Old Controversy." *Civil War History,* Dec. 1982, 293-306.

Colgin, James H. (ed.) "The Life Story of Brig. Gen Felix Robertson." *Texana,* Spring 1970. 154–82.

Cornish, Dudley Taylor. *The Sable Arm: Negro Troops in the Union Army, 1861–1865.* New York: 1956.

Davis, William C. *Breckinridge Statesman Soldier Symbol.* Baton Rouge: 1974.

_____. "Massacre at Saltville." *Civil War Times Illustrated,* Feb. 1971, 4.

Dyer, Brainerd. "The Treatment of Colored Union Troops by the Confederates, 1861–1865." *Journal of Negro History,* July, 1935, 273–86.

Fields, Frank Jr. *28th Virginia Infantry.* Lynchburg, Va: 1985.

Glatthaar, Joseph T. *Forged in Battle: The Civil War Alliance of Black Soldiers and White Officers.* New York: 1991.

Henry, Robert Selph. *"First With the Most" Forrest.* New York: 1944.

Johnson, Robert U. and Buel, Clarence C. (eds.), *Battles and Leaders of the Civil War.* 4 Vols., New York: 1884–1887.

Johnston, J. Stoddard. "Sketches of Operations of General John C. Breckinridge." *The Southern Historical Society Papers,* June–Dec. 1879.

Kent, William B. *A History of Saltville, Virginia*. Radford, Va: 1955.

Lindsley, John Berrien (ed.) *The Military Annals of Tennessee, Confederate*. Nashville: 1886.

Lonn, Ella. *Salt as a Factor in the Confederacy*. New York: 1933.

MacGregor, Morris J. and Natly, Bernard C. (eds.). *Blacks in the United States Armed Forces; Basic Documents*. 2 Vols., Wilmington: 1977.

Marvel, William. "The Battle of Saltville: Massacre or Myth?" *Blue and Gray Magazine*, Aug. 1991, 10–19, 46–60.

_____. *The Battles For Saltville*. Lynchburg, Va.: 1992.

Mason, F.H. *The Twelfth Ohio Cavalry; A record of its Organization, and Services in the War of the Rebellion, Together with a Complete Roster of the Regiment*. Cleveland: 1871.

Mays, Thomas D. "The Price of Freedom: The Battle of Saltville and the Massacre of the Fifth United States Colored Cavalry." Master's Thesis, Virginia Tech. 1992.

McPherson, James M. *The Negro's Civil War*. New York: 1991.

Mosgrove, George Dallas (Bell Wiley ed.). *Kentucky Cavaliers in Dixie: Reminiscences of a Confederate Cavalryman*. Jackson, Tenn: 1957.

Neal, Allen J. *A Bicentennial History of Washington County, Virginia*. Washington, Va: 1977.

Preston, Thomas Lewis. *Historical Sketches and Reminiscences of an Octogenarian*. Richmond: 1900.

Rachal, William M.E. "Salt the South Could Not Savor." *Virginia Cavalcade*, Autumn, 1953.

Robertson, John, comp. *Michigan in the Civil War*. Lansing: 1882.

Robertson, Walter H. "Saltville." *Washington County Historical Society*, March 1943.

Sensing, Thurman. *Champ Ferguson, Confederate Guerilla*. Nashville: 1942.

Smith, Lee. "Experiences of a Kentucky Boy Soldier." *Confederate Veteran,* 1912.

Smyth County Historical Society. *Smyth County-Virginia.* Marion, Va: 1983.

Speed, Thomas. Kelley, R.M. and Pirtle, Alfred. *The Union Regiments of Kentucky.* Lousiville: 1987.

United States War Dept. comp. *War of Rebellion: A Compilation of the Official Records of the Union and Confederate Armies.* 128 Vols. Washington: 1880–1902.

Wilson, Goodridge. *Smyth County History and Traditions.* Kingsport, Tenn: 1932.

Wise, John S. *The End of an Era.* Boston: 1901.

PHOTO CREDITS

We gratefully acknowledge the cooperation of the United States Army Military History Institute at Carlisle Barracks, Pennsylvania, and the assistance of Jim Enos for photographs of John C. Breckinridge, Stephen Gano Burbridge, Basil W. Duke, John Echols, Edward Hobson, Alfred E. "Mudwall" Jackson, Robert Ratliff, Felix H. Robertson, George Stoneman, John S. Williams, a view of Salt Valley, a view of Saltville, Va., and a view of the lower salt-works.

We thank Emory and Henry College for providing a view of the college, *circa* 1874.

We credit the Library of Congress for the photograph of William T. Sherman.

We are grateful to Mr. Gil Barrett for the photograph of Alvan C. Gillem.

For the photographs of Henry Liter Giltner, Edward Guerrant, and George Dallas Mosgrove we credit the book *Kentucky Cavaliers in Dixie* by George Dallas Mosgrove, edited by Bell Irvin Wiley, Broadfoot Publishing Co., Wilmington, N.C., 1991.

For the photograph of Champ Ferguson and guard we credit the book *Champ Ferguson, Confederate Guerilla* by Thurman Sensing, Vanderbilt University Press, 1942.

INDEX